"Claire Weiner has packed an abundance of life into *The Sun Finds Us:* childhood memories, adolescent angst, the adult dramas of romance and marriage, as well as several very moving elegies. Weiner's capacity for creating images and involving us in the stories she tells, as well as the musical qualities of her poems, make reading this book a pleasure. Above all else, these poems speak to us from the heart."

—Richard Tillinghast, author of *Blue If Only I Could Tell You* and *Night Train to Memphis*

"Poet Claire Weiner, in her collection *The Sun Finds Us* writes of love and loss, of the value of a life, of history and its remaining impacts on familial stories, with a tenderness and generosity of heart that infuses all of her work. She portrays details and shifts with a deft and observant eye. In so doing, she brings us to epiphanies of understanding, empathy, and appreciation for the writer's skill. This is a collection I will return to again and again. Weiner's work often includes the wry moment, a touch of humor, or a scathing evaluation of that which ought to be challenged. I am so glad to have her poems close at hand."

-Pia Täavila-Borsheim, Ph.D., author of *Above the Birch Line*

"A profound undercurrent of loss runs through Claire Weiner's new poetry collection, *The Sun Finds Us*, but Weiner transmutes that loss into hope by insisting on the redemptive powers of love and human connection. There's an elegance in her approach to narrative and image that makes reading her poems feel like conversing with a patient and thoughtful friend. It's rare to find a poetic voice this authentic."

-Cal Freeman, author of *The Weather of Our Names*

"Like the varied snapshots of generations of family and friends gone or living, precious moments, and sudden revelations, tender or harsh, Weiner gathers her memories like the stars she gathers for safekeeping for her infant son. While this collection spans a lifetime of thoughtful exploration, and is a necklace of rich and deftly crafted gems each commemorating moments of innocence and/or experience, there is nothing static at all about this book. Each page comes alive with vivid images and turns, as the poems embrace pivotal moments in love like "I think it was a bottle of Zinfandel, but who can remember?" or describe "the scar that no one ever saw" and the "broken, heart/ was repaired/ with harvested/pieces of himself" when the poet talks about her father's struggles, and we trust this voice, especially in these dark times, that claims "Our path is uncharted, but we never lose our way", and that indeed, the sun will find us."

-Zilka Joseph, author of *Sweet Malida: Memories of a Bene Israel Woman, Sparrows and Dust, Sharp Blue Search of Flame*.

The Sun Finds Us

Poems by Claire Weiner

Luchador Press

Big Tuna, Texas

Copyright © Claire Weiner, 2026
First Edition: 1 3 5 7 9 10 8 6 4 2
ISBN: 979-8-89975-035-9
LCCN: 2026933309

Author photo: Joni Strickfaden
Cover image: *Sun Over Olive Grove* by Vincent Van Gogh
Title page image: *Celestial Mechanics* by Detlev Van
    Ravenswaay

Acknowledgments:

I am indebted to the Bear River Writers' Conference in
Northern Michigan, Richard Tillinghast and the poets
in the Monday night group, and to the Hugo House
Alumni group. All wonderful poets and friends.
A special thank you to Zilka Joseph and Pia Borsheim
for their encouragement and poetic wisdom and to
Andy Hansell for her keen eye and decades of
friendship.

And to Kirk, my first reader.

I am grateful to the editors of the following journals,
anthologies and presses in which certain of these poems
appeared, sometimes in slightly different versions or
with different titles:

Muddy River Poetry Review: "August river,"
Lefty Blondie Press 2025 Editor's Choice
    Broadside Series: "The yearling,"
Poet Tree Town Ann Arbor: "The desert,"
Hoffman Center for the Arts: "Finally, spring,"
    "Ode to my husband's hearing aids"
Eclipse, 50th Anniversary Edition: "I mostly knew her
    in her garden,"
Bear River Review: "Ann Arbor alley,"
MacQueens Quinterly: "The weight of newness,"
    "Chicken and eggs,"
Peninsula Poets: "My mother made pickles,"

For a Chance to Walk on Streets of Gold (Finishing Line Press, 2024): "When I was sure of his love," "Talking to the dead,"

Ann Arbor Observer: "And of my tender-hearted son,"

Intima: A Journal of Narrative Medicine: "What adults say and do when your daughter has cancer,"

The Write Launch, 2025: "my first time", "The Sun Finds Us," "My Boyfriend and I Drive from Bloomington to Champaign, 1978,"

Aorta Literary Magazine (forthcoming): Sometimes it felt like my father was held together by scars

Table of Contents:

Slowing Down

In the World

For my parents, who I wish were alive to read these poems.
For my children—Nathan, Iveta, Anna and Jonathan.
For Samuel who lights up the world.
And always, for Kirk.

Slowing Down

Learning to meditate

For months, I sit, cross-legged on a cushion
surrounded by others who sit
as stone statues

appear to be in states of Buddha-bliss
eyes closed, corners
of their mouths uplifted.

But I am fidgety as a preschooler
and my thoughts
skitter like leaves in a November wind.

Surely, I'm failing at this thing called meditation.

The teacher, her voice soothing and silvery,
uses metaphors
and similes, as often as white clover blooms in July.

Imagine your breath as a floating anchor.
The wandering mind is a puppy.

I begin to notice, that, even as my mind
still dances,
like kernels of corn in hot oil, I care less—

disappointments, imperfections,
and longings begin to shift

behind a scrim— replaced by a love affair
with the everyday: Yellow daylilies spreading sunlight

along a graveled road, the snuffles and snores
of my old dog curled near the radiator. I watch

regrets recede like spring floodwaters. And watch
as they reappear with the next storm.

August river

My kayak's yellow paddle carves

the river's water, divides its green rippled

surface in a sculpture

of perpetual motion.

River grass   and   sedge blow in a slow

and easy current

rocks glisten

like gems

beneath the surface

jeweled dragonflies just above.

The day simply clamors for my attention

I struggle to be everywhere at once.

And there, in the shade of a lumbering willow,

wades a heron, patient, and precise.

The yearling

I feel her before I see her on a June
      afternoon glutted with humidity.

She steps from behind her sanctuary
      of trembling aspen and river birch

onto the pavement—the distance
      between us mere yards.

She moves like a dancer, with small leaps,
      her hooves silent as they settle.

I'd been alone on the path lost in a tangle
      of damp thoughts when she appeared.

Perhaps, I might have closed the gap
      between us if I'd noticed her sooner.

I might have tried to earn her trust, touched
      her wiry fur before she floated back
      into her wooded refuge.

I might have followed.

The desert

I travel to the desert
where turquoise sky overflows with sun.

Clear-eyed, I watch for scorpions
and rattlesnakes on quiet dusty paths.

I'm nourished by spaciousness
of earth and heaven.

Few visitors arrive.

But I greet them with gladness,
for although I crave the quiet and the sun,

I also crave the company.

Bonsai master

—for G.

Alone now, she will wait
for unfolding sunsets on the crystal
waters of her lake. She will shift

her gaze from window to shore
to window, and from room to room.
She will observe white and gray

kingfishers hover, then dive into the mirrored
surface. She will still hear her husband's
voice in the kitchen, think she sees him

slicing pork roast, pouring drinks—Martini
for him, Manhattan with a twist for her.

She will watch him in their well-tended garden,
bending over the 100-year-old
juniper with tiny pliers, scissors and

bamboo rakes the size of his hand.

A long-ago unexplained death

—for Julie

Sometimes, as I hike high in the Catalinas,
along Blackett's Ridge I look down and
remember your backflips.

How you windmilled across the glossy grain
of the maple gym floor. Your blonde ponytail
whipping every which way

your bangs flying skyward. How you landed
solidly as an oak. Every time.
A bit breathless, with a wide white smile.

Fifty years later, I wake early, and while still warm
beneath the covers, ponder clues as I work a word
puzzle. At an outdoor music festival, under a cloudless

canopy, I'll listen to the sounds of an oldies rock band.
and end my day watching my grandson
eat an orange, juice dripping down his chin & chest.

You and I were barely eighteen when you took
the lead along a steep trail in the Rockies, disappearing
around a bend.

Did you really take a misstep that day?

The bench

—for Jennie who was gifted a park bench for her 70th birthday

And some time make the time to sit
on Jennie's bench. Beyond a wooden
bridge lies the narrow, shaded footpath.
Turn onto it from the wide brazen meadow.
Listen to the sound of your steps, as you
straddle twisted tree roots, walk upon layers
of leaves among a shadowed slit in the woods.
There, among maple, honey locust, and sycamore
the bench rests, waits for your arrival, waits
for you to settle with yourself. The river
shimmers, the woods reassure. You have
all the time you need.

After Seamus Heaney

I mostly knew her in her garden
—for Valerie

    as she bent over peonies or lilies,
cutting an errant
leaf or withering petal, tending each
as though they
were her one of her three children.

Sometimes, we'd find each other
at the park,
each of us with our dogs—hers a purebred
mine a mixed
breed. The meetings, never on purpose

always pleasant. Our dogs played until breathless.
Together, we might
walk the short distance back to our
neighboring houses
chatting about weather or her grandson.

When I learned she fell ill, I rang her doorbell
stood on her stoop
with a container of vegetable soup. She opened
the door a crack,
thanked me with a broken smile. Her dog silent in the
background.

The next day, the empty container returned
to my stoop.
A scrawled thank you inside.
A pattern repeated many times,
until, one day the container was not returned.

I last saw her early this spring,
securing tendrils
of a golden
clematis vine
to a trellis,
making
sure
it was
safe.

Late May

Together, we walk through my spring garden
         take our time turning
leaf and petal, large and small.

Iris are impossible to ignore,
         towering above all else, loud
and purple, shout *look at us, look at us.*

Lilacs draw us in with their quiet
         gauziness, almost indecent
scent, whisper, *come closer, come closer.*

Roses snag us, an extravagance of scarlet
         buds set to explode like unannounced
fireworks, its thorns remind us, *don't touch.*

Lamb's Ear, so soft, so close to the earth
         caught her eye and made her kneel
to stroke a leaf as if it were the hand of sleepy baby.

How I miss

all the letters and emails I no longer receive
because some parts of your brain have
ceased to function, resulting in great
difficulty gathering memories & words.
Even walking, slowly, arm-in arm, you
fear missteps, want to remain close, with a
gait— uncertain, hesitant. How deeply you
hope for what is damaged-beyond-repair
inside your skull to be restored,
joined together, like the plastic model car
kits glued as a boy, or the '57 Corvette you
loved driving in the leafy suburb you never
moved from. You used to laugh at your
neuroses, years on the couch, but not now.
Once upon a time you wanted to change
professions—leave advertising. But you
quickly returned to jingle-writing. You
realized your talent! But, one day your heart
seized, your head hit concrete with a soft
thud & words like napkin, nose, elude you.
Undone, by your wounded brain, you try
valiantly to recall the color of your Celica,
where we hiked on the California coast, the
exact chord progression in Rescue Me.

Your perfect timing, your turn of phrase, your
zany impressions of Donald Duck—
    oh, how I miss them all.

Finally, spring

Morning, muffled by moisture,
hangs like overripe fruit.

Sweat soaks into my faded *Illinois*
t-shirt.

Two dozen waxy-leafed begonias
wait patiently to spread their roots,

their ruby blossoms sway
like tiny wings as I set them

on top of a Midwestern jumble
of clay and glacial till.

I push aside old mulch, sweep
desiccated roots, displace

crickets and stink bugs, work
the soil with my gloved hands

until it finally feels like bread
flour between my fingers.

I remove the plants from
their too-small-black-plastic pots

massage their roots, and finally
place them in the space

where they can flourish
until first frost.

A call

I wake to a day, gray and damp
as old gym clothes stuffed
in the back of a closet.

Staying in bed seems reasonable.

But above mutterings of my morning
mind, I hear a quiet call of the climbing
rose bush outside my window

as it winds over and under the old
wooden trellis its bound to with twisties
from Buy Rite. Its blossoms, when new,

are the color of a fine Merlot. But now,
they've faded, and look like coffee
left in the glass carafe at the end

of a day. Such unsightliness wrestles
me out of bed, and out the door,
where in spite of myself

I'm lost, deadheading,
among green things and thorns.

In the World

Going steady, seventh grade

His blond hair escaped his Brylcreem.
His silver toned I.D bracelet jingled on
his wrist. His blue eyes stealthily darted
towards my desk during class. He was tall,
lean, and wore tight black pants. I was
brunette, petite, blue-eyed. I wore a blue
plaid jumper and a white blouse. My gold,
six-pointed star hung from a delicate chain
around my neck. Our last names were
already chummy—mine began with a *W*
and his with a *V*—so we were often
coupled together in class projects. When
we leaned against the cold metal locker in
the Honors Hallway that late Friday afternoon,
I held my breath. When as he asked, *"Do you
want to go steady?"* I said, "*Of* course, yes!"
I turned as red as the hearts I drew in my
notebook with his name and mine. I heard
the small click of his I.D. bracelet as he opened
it, another click as he placed it on my wrist.
Now, I was wearing *Christopher.* I thought
forever. I raced home, threw open the back
door, into the Sabbath aroma of my mother's
kitchen. Soup simmering, chicken roasting,
and candles set out for lighting. She spotted
the silver bracelet, sighed deeply, shook her head.
"My shayne maidel and a Christopher. Never."

Ruby Tuesday

Danny DeAngelo doesn't date short Jewish
girls like me. Everyone knows he's in love
with Marina Marelli—a teen-aged Sophia Loren.
But that doesn't stop me from doodling his
name all over my spiral notebooks, or dreaming
about his slicked-back, jet-black hair, bulging
biceps, skin-tight pants and greaser, pointy toed
shoes with enough of a heel to click, click,
click as he struts down the hall. After months
of me flirting with him, despite friends' warnings
to *Stay away from Danny; you don't stand a
chance*, he asks me out. Danny DeAngelo,
high school junior, guitar player, drummer, and
driver of a second-hand car without a muffler,
walks by me in the hall, turns and says, "Let's
go to Il Forno. You eat pizza, right? Friday, okay?"
My head bounces up and down as fast as my
beating heart.

He honks his rumbling Rambler, and I run out
the door before my parents can ask questions.
Ruby Tuesday is playing on the car radio. "I love
this song, don't you", I gush. Danny wordlessly
shrugs. I've been playing *Ruby Tuesday* on my
record player in my bedroom for weeks. *Lose
your dreams and you will lose your mind* has
become my personal mantra. I lose my mind
every time Mick shakes his tambourine.

As we sit down on the red leatherette booth
at the restaurant, our thighs momentarily
slide against each other. I think, so what if
Danny doesn't love Mick's tambourine or
Ruby Tuesday as much as I do. Our hands
almost brush as we reach across the checked
tablecloth for the menus. I'm convinced I've
found my own dream right here, alongside
Danny. We order cheese pizza and Coke,
and I sit staring into his eyes, waiting for him
to say something.

"I really like pizza", he says, "You're a Jewish girl,
aren't you?" "I've never been out with a Jewish girl
before. I guess I didn't know Jews ate pizza!"
I nearly spurt a mouthful of Coke on the table.
"I didn't mean nothing by it." "It's just my grandma,
I call her Nona, says Jewish people don't eat pizza.
They don't eat a lot of other stuff either—like ham
sandwiches, cheeseburgers, lasagna." I'm speechless.
Danny keeps going, "Do you really not eat lasagna?
I mean, *no* lasagna? That would be tough." Danny
is interrupted when the waitress places the hot,
steaming pizza on the table.

I grab a slice, jam it into my mouth, ignoring the
burn of the melted, stringy, cheese. I barely finish
the first slice when I grab a second. "Whoa," Danny
says, his eyes wide, "I guess my grandma was wrong."
Before I take a bite from the second slice, I manage

to spit out, "Right. Your grandma is definitely wrong.
There's a whole lot you and your, whatever, don't
know about me. And I guess even more that I
don't know about you."

Danny sits and stares as I finish chewing.

"Maybe you should tell your Nona to listen to *Ruby
Tuesday*. And you can listen with her while you're at it."
I motion to the waitress, "I'll take the rest of this pizza
to go. Can you put it in a box, please?"

Danny sits there, his eyes wider than before, a piece of
pizza uneaten on his plate. I grab that piece of uneaten
pizza from Danny's plate and put it in the pizza box,
my pizza box. I walk with my box and my emergency
quarters to the phone booth at the front of Il Forno
and call my parents to pick me up. They'll be happy
to share the pizza with me.

Afternoon bridge game, 1960

I'm home from fifth grade with a headache. I went
back to sleep for a while before my mother brought me
her sick bed specialty— milk tea, a soft-boiled egg, and
cinnamon toast. She left me in my room with *Half
Magic* and *Zlateh the Goat,* two of my favorite books,
along with crackers, apple juice, and a small silver bell
to jingle "just in case". She reminds me that her *girlfriends*
are coming to play bridge. I hear Mom in the kitchen
for a while, but when the doorbell starts ringing, I
stop reading and move quietly from my bedroom to
a perch at the top of the stairs where I'm unnoticed.
I watch my mother's friends, all well-coiffed and well-
girdled, greet each other with ease. They take their seats
without delay, in our living room, where the gold-colored
sofa and two olive green occasional chairs, bought on
lay-a-way, have been rearranged to make room for the
card table set. There are small bowls of nuts and hard
candies. The scent of an artificial pine forest mingles
with Eau de Joy and Shalimar, heightened by the warmth
of the women' s pulse points. Cards are dealt quickly,
they know the game must end before they hear the shifting
gears of the # 8 school bus at the end of the street.
My older sister and all the neighbor kids will be on that
bus. My mom's friend Shirley ponders her bid, her scarlet
fingertips thrum the table. Evelyn does the same with
hers, frosted white. Bev, tired of waiting asks, "What's
your story, morning glory?" with a little

laugh, and my mother opens her pack of Lucky Strikes. Matches are struck, cigarettes lit, smoke inhaled, and the room suddenly becomes quiet. My mother and her friends look like they're somewhere else. I don't make a sound. What's going on, I wonder. Then I remember something my sister told me. "Sometimes when mom looks like she's far away, she's lost in her memories of before she was our mom, of before she knew dad, of time during the big war." I wonder if that's happening now to my mom and her bridge partners. I know they met each other and became friends when they worked together in an airplane factory. It's hard to imagine them working in a factory, wearing overalls, and work gloves, their hair tied up in kerchiefs. But my mother has shown me pictures and shown me places in our big World Atlas where my father, Uncle Jerry, and my best friend Margie's father were during the war. Mom told me she and her friends had to learn where Guadalcanal, Saipan and Kursk were, and how to pronounce those faraway places. How she and her friends prayed for their brothers and sweethearts to come home.

my first time, 1968

—for a boy named alan

in the basement
of the bi-level
where I live
with my parents
and older sister
in a small middle class
suburb of Chicago
while my parents
are upstairs
watching carol burnett
he and I struggle with
our unformed selves

he is so different
from the usual boys
jocks cool dressers
he is pure nerd

but there is a certain
je ne sais quoi
about him
his cardigan
his suede elbow patches
his rusty two-door
ford falcon

so that when he places
his trembling sixteen-year-old
sweaty hand
on my padded
maidenform *chasonette* bra
i feel the full strength
of his steeliness

we don't last much
beyond
that basement grope

but he teaches me
so much about
e.e. cummings

no caps.

My boyfriend and I drive from Bloomington
to Champaign, 1970
—after Cal Freeman

Insects glut our windshield like Saturday confessions
at Our Lady of the Prairie on a day

so sapped by humidity our car
seems to lose speed. Radio stations sputter,

the backs of our thighs slowly melt into cracked
vinyl seats, as searing air blasts

through open windows of our '59 Chevy.
Desiccated cornfields line the road. It's a helluva

drive after a wrecked weekend with friends
who never missed a chance to swipe or gripe

at each other about God-knows. We skipped out
before the kill, before the weekend devolved

into something like The Ride of the Valkyries.
Now, we're pushing the pedal to make it home

before nightfall, when a station, maybe in Terre Haute,
decides to cue Pachelbel's Canon in D Major.

The violins and cello settle over us
and we pull to the side of the rode to listen,
corn stalks rustling.

Why I want to remember summer

Shorty pajamas and crop tops
learning to twirl a baton at day camp
running a sack race
   with a boy I liked, until we won and he tried
   to kiss me

Condensation dripping off our aluminum water pitcher
my father supine on the patio lounge
Hitachi transistor radio atop his chest
   Luis Aparicio stealing one after another for the
   White Sox

Still summer nights, my older sister and friends letting me
play *Concentration* with them at our kitchen table,
root beer floats and potato chips with sour cream dip
   made by our mother
   and sometimes she joined in

The kids of the 7300 block of North Kilbourne Avenue
running behind a DDT truck as it sprayed its swelling
cloud of sweet smelling chemical
   once or twice
   all summer long

In August my best friend and I doused our bikinied
bodies with baby oil, covered her father's double
Buddy Rich albums with foil and reflected sun
   onto our pale Midwestern skin
   frying it to a perfect glow

My friends and I singing, *we all want to change the world*
over and over with the lads from Liverpool,
as we lay on hot rough sand at Morse Beach,
        at the edge of a Great Lake—
        We believed every word was true.

The morning after my 40th
high school reunion

I drive my rental car onto Kilbourne Avenue,
the route home embroidered deep within me.

Maples mix with oaks and lindens, span the
street with an unrestrained canopy of green and gold.

I park at the north end of the pavement.

There, we're playing "Border Game", crossing
the invisible line where Mark, Ellen and I sneak
over on bikes. Jail is beyond the tangle of buckthorn
and honeysuckle.

At the south end, is the corner where we're waiting
for the hiss and groan of the school bus. Yes, even
on winter mornings, when Chicago wind
whips you like you've done something wrong.

My front yard, where I sat in the shade of the stately
sycamore and read Nancy Drews has vanished,
replaced by an asphalt driveway. The white-barked
birch faithfully guard my small second-story bedroom.

My parents are still in the kitchen on their endless loop
of worries about money and my father's lack
of get-up-and-go.

I press my hand against the hollowed kitchen door,
wish it was filled with something besides my parents'
unhappiness.

Maybe with something like tenderness or love.

Ann Arbor alley

No one thinks to tend the pavement
where we walk daily, where the grit and gristle
of winter is yet underfoot, caught in cold torrents

of early spring rain as it engorges
gutters. Here, downspouts are overwhelmed
and cigarette butts turn to spongy

afterthoughts. I tread lightly through slush, past
bus boys speaking their mother's tongues, delivery
trucks spewing bits of invisible poison.

Tattooed hairdressers huddle under eaves—
clandestine smokers trying to defy early death.
I step over shards of last night's celebrations—

discards of hoped-for-love, splinters of glass,
used condoms— to my office three flights up.

We spoke of marriage, 1980

Was it a bottle of Zinfandel, who can remember?
You were on a business trip to L.A., to film an ad
for Buick, perhaps Pontiac, on the Malibu coast.
Malibu is ash and dust now. It was dazzling then.

You were on a business trip to L. A. We plunged
our Midwest bodies into the surf, rode the waves.
Malibu is ash and dust now. It was dazzling then.
I wore a bikini, mostly strings the color of sea glass.

We plunged our Midwest bodies into the surf
rode the waves. Your fair skin turned to burnt toast.
I wore a bikini, mostly strings the color of sea glass.
We spoke quietly about marriage—yours, mine.

Your fair skin had turned to burnt toast.
We drove to my place a few miles from the beach.
We spoke quietly of marriage—
yours now always disharmonic, the finale of mine.

We drove to my place a few miles from the beach.
You said, "I can't be the bad guy."
Your marriage now always disharmonic.
I said, "There's not always a bad guy."

You sat on my couch, "I can't be the bad guy. "
I played Tom Waits on my turntable.
There's not always a bad guy.
We opened another bottle, but who can remember.

My Parents

Chickens and eggs

Like the stool she perches on at the outdoor
market, the egg lady's face is weathered. But
her farm-fresh eggs nestle neatly
into hollows of assorted cartons.
She explains,
> *I call my hens by their names.*
> *Each and every one of my girls.*

I buy two dozen, twice what I need.

Retired, my grandfather, an immigrant tailor
from Poland, bought a poultry farm in California.
Longing for light after a lifetime of stitching in half-light,
He too loved his hens, named them—
> *Golda, Shayna, Chana.*

Each one named for someone left behind.

Frank lived next door to us with Fannie and their three
sons. Every morning, he drove to his poultry shop where
he and his brother killed chickens all day—the kosher
  way.
Friday mornings, my mother would call across
the path,

> *Frank, bring home a sweet girl for me. Oh, and*
> *a nice dozen.*

At the end of the day, Frank, stepped into our kitchen
     with blood-splattered
apron, delivered a package to our kitchen counter.
     Still warm.

My mother made pickles

In the soggy heat of Chicago summers,
        my mother carried two brown crocks
                from the basement.

She hosed them off on our small patio,
        removed dust and dead spiders, set them
                to dry on the concrete stoop.

They were nothing like the Royal Rose
        gold-trimmed dinner plates
                she used for special occasions,

yet she handled these cumbersome,
        coarse, containers
                with the same great care.

She filled them with cucumbers
        the length of her hand,
                perfect, but unmeasured amounts of spice.

She set an everyday salad plate atop
        each crock, sent me to find a rock
                to secure the plate.

"Fermentation takes time," she said.
        I think she was telling me
                to be patient.

We checked the burgeoning pickles day to day.
We removed the cover, skimmed mystery foam
returned the crock's contents to
darkness.

She knew the exact moment
the transformation was complete.
One jar went to our neighbors

Fanny and Frank. The rest
were eaten before the fireflies
ceased to light up the August sky.

My father, sister and I relished the crunch, the tang,
and bite of garlic in each of my mother's pickles.

But my mother never took a bite,
she said they didn't agree
with her.

Daily check-in

Your face dappled in shadow as you sit on your small
Miami balcony wearing a pink & blue flowered

robe. You drink coffee, black, eat toast, lightly
buttered, work the first or second of many crossword

puzzles. A morning show drones. Your phone screams,
flashes, like an ambulance, until you answer.

We discuss your hands, how they ache from years
of knitting, a tender hip. "I woke before dawn again."

Your plans for the day. You thank me for calling,
        "Of course, why wouldn't I?"
        "Well, not all daughters do, you know."

You return to your puzzles; I park behind my office
building, walk slowly up three flights.

Do you remember when we gathered shells at South
Beach?
You always spotted sand dollars first, bleached white
by the sun.

The bagel place

My sister and I drove to the bagel place,
sat in a red vinyl booth facing a parking lot.

Florida's July heat already shimmering
off black asphalt. I nodded when the waitress

offered coffee, pointed to the picture of scrambled
eggs on the menu. My sister muttered, "The same."

92-year-old kidneys don't last forever,
even in our mother.

Six months before, she declined dialysis.
"Throwing good money after bad," she'd said,

as though talking to a car mechanic instead of the
white-coated specialist at the foot of her hospital bed.

He didn't disagree.

And so, we flew home, waited until her knees buckled—
the phone call came, burst the fantasy of our mother's
immortality.

We sat by her side for five days.

Her breath grew more ragged, less substantial, her blue
eyes more clouded, her hands less open.

But on that last day, when I lingered,
alone with her in the hospice room,
her cheeks were as soft as ever.

To my father

As you lay dying in the sweltering
Miami summer, I stayed home,

cooled by an offshore breeze
in Santa Monica. When I visited you two weeks

before, my son against my breast,
you who delighted in babies more than anything,

could barely raise your arm to do
the disappearing-nose-trick.

I couldn't bear to see you yet again, held
together with plastic tubing and manufactured

oxygen, accompanied by the low
hum of machines. You, who loved Caruso, Callas,

Shuman and Shubert, once told me the sound
of the hospital was D minor. You, who were my

favorite parent, a secret I kept to myself, not even
daring to write it in my diary with the tiny gold lock.

Not even daring to tell you.

Sometimes it felt like my father
was held together by scars

The ropy scar
on his back,
the one from before
I was born—
leathery
and snake-like
the one
my mother
talked
about so often
and with such fervor,
I could see
the surgeon
cut through skin,
then fascia and muscle,
finally reaching
my father's twisted
and tortuous esophagus
to liberate it
from itself.

And the small, serrated scar
on his right knee
that would never again
push the suburban
lawnmower,

or bowl
with his buddies
on Thursday nights,
or golf
on Sunday mornings.
The knee that would
forever be braced
and swollen.

The long
straight
scar, red
and raised,
that came
from flaying
his torso
like a kosher

cut of beef,
as his true,
broken, heart
was repaired
with harvested
pieces of himself.

The scar that no one
ever saw
but that followed
my father, and his father
who fled a small

speck on a map
somewhere
between Kyiv and Minsk,
a scar—
invisible
like mold
until you notice it,
black and menacing.

My father, a lion

Today I'm longing for my father,
the undamaged one

the one without wounds
from poundings on his worn-out chest

or the one who didn't surrender
33 times to an intensive care bed.

No, I'm longing for the father in this photo
before I was born, standing tall,

sleek, at attention, in khaki
and olive-drab in front of an imposing

limestone building, as if he were a four-star
general, Secretary of State or maybe of War.

But now, when I look closely
I see he is standing on the steps of the Art Institute
of Chicago

but the famous bronze lions, one defiant,
one on the prowl are barely
outside the frame.

Talking to the dead

My oldest friend talks
to her dead parents. Calls
them by their first names—
Bobbie and Sam.

Her house overflows
with their Coltrane & Mingus,
tablecloths, wooden
salad bowl, silver candlesticks.

She hears their laughs, feels
warmth around their oak table.
Sees Sam guide Bobbie
across the dance floor,

his hand gentle on her back,
her head at home on his
shoulder, how he never missed
a chance to sweep her off her feet.

Her home is papered with photographs
of them—windowsills, dresser
tops, refrigerator magnets—
in the blush of first love, wizened with age.

She never misses a chance
to light a candle or sanctify
their memory.

But I don't remember my parents
in silver-filigreed frames,
with stuff on shelves, faded letters
of devotion bound with ribbons in a drawer.

Long ago I stopped collecting
memories, saying blessings.

Yet, when *I lie down and when I rise up,*

I see my mother's wrist— gold
charms jangling, my father's hands

gliding the bow of his violin —
towards the slow echo of Barber's *Adagio for Strings.*

Takes on Love

When I was sure of his love
—for Kirk

And when I was sure enough
of his heart's goodness, I told
him the story of my father,
the gentlest of souls.

I told him of jokes mailed
to comedians—Jack Benny, Jerry Lewis,
Milton Berle and the rest—and autographed thank-yous
in return.

I told him of contraband Cuban cigars,
Saturday afternoons at the opera in basement-
turned-rec room, playing poker for frilled
toothpicks, backrubs when I was sick,

and of blueberry pancakes on Sunday
mornings—just us two early risers—
of forbidden ham and cheese on Jewish rye
and the Odyssean search for perfect coleslaw.

I told of my father who sat too often
in the living room chair—
praying for ambition that was always just out of reach,
how my mother didn't understand.

And of the long, crooked scar on my father's back,
the small one on his knee, the life-saving ones
on his thigh and chest where they switched out
bad artery for good suddenly one Monday morning.

I told him of the endless night that descended
on my father after he was brought back
from the dead that Monday, how my sister and I
visited him in a psych ward. My mother too
    defeated to go.

I told him of my father's apology, so hushed we
could barely hear, his eyes overflowed
with shame. In the elevator my sister
and I hugged and sobbed. I was twenty-one.

When I finished unraveling
the tale of my father, he looked
at me with the gentleness
of dawn.

Then, I was sure.
And we lay together.

The weight of newness

—for my son

Your slightest cry ripples through me.
Rising from the light sleep of motherhood,

I find you tucked in flannelled shadows,
gather you and feel the weight of newness.

Blanketing you with my robed body, I pad
into the room at the top of the stairs.

Night after night, from late winter
through spring, we sit cocooned

on the brown tweed couch, fighting sleep,
watching our reflections in the sliding glass door.

We breathe in the brine and salt of the Pacific.
Distant misty foghorns and shushing waves soothe us.

I wrap you in another blanket and another,
and we step out into the cool California night.

The stars flicker through swaying eucalyptus,
so close I can touch them.

I gather them for your safekeeping.

And of my tender-hearted son

On the cusp of fall, on a path along
the Huron River, where sumac
and dogwood entwine in flaming dance,

aspen and hickory compete for best
in show, I meet the Buddha.

He bows. And of course, so do I. Then,
in his gentle Buddha-way, he instructs
me to think of death.

Not once. But many times. He places
his hand, soft as milkweed moth,
on my shoulder.

Cessation, stillness and unflinching
gray will descend. I notice a small knot
in my chest, a tighter one in my belly.
.

He follows, his silence supporting
me. I think about my parents—

my father singing with Pavarotti
in the paneled family room, my mother
crocheting intricate blankets. Both

always worrying about money. Both
always loving me. I think of my husband
of forty years—the heat of youth,

the balm of old age. And of my tender-hearted
son who makes all numbers add up,
and my daughter who dances with each day.

And of my grandson who places Matchbox cars
under his pillow, dreams about a world filled with string
cheese and pretzels.

The resplendence will end.

I shake my head, yet I know it is
the truth.

What adults say and do when your
12-year-old has cancer

From spring into summer into fall, all you can
do is walk in a straight line.

Your secretary gets teary, gives a limp
hug. The scout leader sends

a sad-eyed emoji. The well-intentioned,
God-blessing neighbors bring flowers

and cheesy casseroles, with sweet notes
reminding to *please return* their Williams Sonoma

dish. Never do you eat their food. Never do they think
their flowers need to be watered. Bouquets droop

and scatter onto the dining room table, where no one
has eaten for months.

The nurses will call you "Mom."

You will protect this child whose head
is now smooth as sea glass, who asks, "Why me."

You will remember playing beauty shop,
braiding her honey-colored hair, tying her braids

with big bows & small, painting her fingers & toes.
She painted yours the most shocking pink.

You will look up and remember, she is not
the only child. A 15-year-old son is waiting patiently.

He is also watching to see what you're really made of.
Because he too, is trying to find out what he's really

made of, when his sister, who he hates, but also loves,
is so sick he has to carry her down the stairs.

A mother like me

"A walnut-sized lump on a daughter's neck is nothing
to fear," except for a mother like me.

Forty-page treatment protocols for a 12-year-old
become bedside reading for a mother like me.

Question after question to oncologist, surgeon, nurse,
always end with, "Are you a parent like me?"

Scrutinize anemic daughter's blood counts—they
hold the key for a mother like me. Demand reason

for demerit given to bald daughter who wears hat
in 7th grade. Be ferocious, omnipresent like me.

Carry a red notebook to record side effects, symptoms
fevers. Become a compulsive medical editor like me.

Carry the full weight of your thin-as-a-rake daughter,
because you would do anything as a mother like me.

"Don't say this is a weird virus, bronchitis or any
    other itis."
Something deadly, a mother like me can see with clarity.

Ode to my king-size mattress

How I dream of each encounter
with you. I relax onto you,
night after night and nap after nap,

you ensure my slumber is sound,
and sweet as the first Red Globe peach
picked in Michigan in July.

No matter how heavy my eyes, or how sore
my limbs, you embrace me with utter
tenderness, make each awakening a joy

like a most reliable and selfless lover,
asking so little in return, only that, twice a year—
when crocus appear, and when trees begin to show

their nakedness, I flip you over, giving
you a chance to breathe. And though some
might think this a difficult task,

given your thickness and royalty,
I'm eager to do it, to repay you in some small
way, because of everything you do for me.

After all, I nestle nightly next to my one true love
in your organic wool, latex and cotton. Yes, there have
been other mattresses before, but none

compare with your unparallelled blend
of gentleness and support, the way you uphold
your commitment to me each and every time
I seek your comfort.

Ode to my husband's hearing aids

Sorcerer of sound, Eros
whose arrow points directly
into my beloved's ears,
I adore you.

Minuscule, featherweight, miracle!
Resting so lightly on the flesh of ear canals,
transmiting sound in a way utterly beyond me.

You perform your magic so quietly.
No cheering crowds, no minions in the
in the wings. In fact, you do your
meticulous work while camouflaged.

You gather my words
instantaneously, convert them
into mysterious codes.
You amplify them, loud as a giant.

Then, you sweep your magic wand,
codes become waves, rush into his ears
pulse through curlicue canals, bang
into a drum, dance through an elaborate
labyrinth of hammer, anvil, stirrup,
end in a snail touched by a special nerve.

Our forty-year conversation continues
at the well-worn oak dining table in Michigan
or under a sprawling Palo Verde in Tucson,
without a "huh" or "what."

If not for you, our long love affair might have
shattered, not for change of heart, but for
change of hearing. All my sweet nothings
turned to sweet nothing.

Ode to my husband's CPAP machine

Oh, sleep savior, snore
stopper, I salute the sweet
hiss of your carefully calibrated

continuous pressure. I applaud
your lifesaving, heart-saving,
finely, filtered currents

as they flow through tiny, plastic,
conduits that rest like petite
pillows on my husband's nostrils.

So, what if I wake from a dream
about a freight train
or tsunami, only to realize

what I'm hearing is the
whoosh-whoosh and whistle
escaping from you,

a machine, the size of a two-slice
toaster on my sweetheart's
nightstand. And who cares

if your pliable corrugated tubing
loosens and flails in the night
like an asthmatic ghost's arm?

With the perfect amount
of propulsion you keep
my beloved's airways open.

You nourish his brain and heart,
with all the oxygen necessary for him to think
about and love me, til death do us part.

After Thanksgiving, a love poem

They depart and the day slips too slowly
into evening. They've flown back

to their grown-up homes, digital check books
and to-do lists, their Smartwool socks

with holes in the heels. Now, we're without
our daughter's gracefulness, as she tenderly

scoops up her toddler, settles him
on the couch to read about rockets, again.

And without our son's dazzling blue eyes
that see the world with quickness

and generosity—a combination that never
fails to soften my heart.

He is off, hand-in-hand with his love to hike
the hills of Patagonia. And she and her husband's

days are filled with wooden blocks,
and trains named Thomas.

When I hold my children close, I know their worlds
are no longer mine.

You will play guitar. I will write poems.

We stand at the window, watch wild turkeys
strut across the field. We laugh about snoods
and wattles.

Remembering goodness

Thank you, I whisper to no one,
as I open my eyes, find my breath, listen

for his. I rest my hand quietly on the blue
quilted comforter, sculpted over his still, slumbering

body, leave bed with a morning's stiffness I've come
to expect, and steep the first pot of tea

from our garden's mint. I've begun this ritual
of saying thank you, each morning.

Is it gratitude or am I trying to hold on to what I have?

Once, we lingered long mornings, like cats in the sun
licking and mewing with pleasure, our limbs tangled.

We couldn't see an end.

With children, bed was a thing we fell onto—
for as long as our son and daughter, like baby
birds with mouths open, allowed.

We couldn't see an end.

For a while, we were disoriented, came to bed
only after caring for others. Our animal bodies worn,
unable to hear each other's sighs or cries.

We couldn't see an end.

Tonight, we stand on our deck, pretend to identify
constellations we can barely discern. We fall,
laughing onto our bed.

The sun finds us

In my mustard-colored Toyota, we drive
    from the smoggy city, its over-trafficked
    hallways, hike in ocean-misted hills,
        ripe with red-stemmed manzanita.

Our path is uncharted, but we never lose
    our way, never lose sight of the wavering
        ocean below. We let its irregularities guide
        us, imagine its underwater mysteries.

And there, on a wooden bench, dedicated
    to someone who once loved the view, I take
    you by surprise. You, so unable to resist.
        And there, only the sun finds us.

Claire Weiner was born in Chicago and raised in the Chicago suburbs by parents who were profoundly affected by the previous generation of Jews who left Europe in search of a better life. Her childhood was permeated with stories of the old country and the specter of antisemitism. With the exception of ten years in Los Angeles, she has spent most of her adult life in Ann Arbor, Michigan where she and her husband raised their son and daughter. She spent her decades-long non-writing career as a clinical social worker, helping people make more sense of their life stories. She began writing in earnest when her son and daughter were grown. She and her husband now split their time between Ann Arbor and Tucson, grateful to be part of vibrant university communities in both places. Her first book, a chapbook, *For a Chance to Walk on Streets of Gold* was published in 2024. Her poetry and flash fiction has been published widely.

This project was made possible, in part, by generous support from the Osage Arts Community.

Osage Arts Community provides temporary time, space and support for the creation of new artistic works in a retreat format, serving creative people of all kinds — visual artists, composers, poets, fiction and nonfiction writers. Located on a 152-acre farm in an isolated rural mountainside setting in Central Missouri and bordered by ¾ of a mile of the Gasconade River, OAC provides residencies to those working alone, as well as welcoming collaborative teams, offering living space and workspace in a country environment to emerging and mid-career artists. For more information, visit us at www.osageac.org

www.ingramcontent.com/pod-product-compliance
Lightning Source LLC
Chambersburg PA
CBHW020456160726

47991CB00007B/2677